101
Things *to*
Dislike 👎
About Facebook

Gary Gusick

No part of this book may be reproduced, stored in a retrieval system, or transmitted in any form by any means, electronic, mechanical, photocopying, recording or otherwise, without written permission from the publisher, except brief excerpts quoted for the purpose of review.

Copyright © 2012 Gary Cusick
All rights reserved
Published by Benoit Press

ACKNOWLEDGEMENTS
The author would like to thank the following people for their contributions to this effort: Lee Ann Mayo, James Neidorf, Nicole Stowe for cover and graphic design, and Anthony Vachris.

Millions of people the world over think
Facebook is the greatest thing that ever happened.

This book is dedicated to the rest of us.

===

1.

PEOPLE WITH DOZENS OF PROFILE PHOTOS THAT ALL LOOK THE SAME

2.
You can't un-friend someone unless you friend them first

3.
Five minutes on Facebook
can feel like an hour
in the greeting card section
at Walgreens

4.
Photos of cats and dogs dressed in funny outfits

**5.
You're connected to
643 people you
don't actually know and
don't really want to**

6.
Mark Zuckerberg's character in *The Social Network* never apologized to the girl from BU for posting that she wasn't a C cup

7.

YOU DISCOVER PHOTOS OF
YOURSELF MAKING OUT
AT THE OFFICE CHRISTMAS PARTY

8.
Your boss discovers the same photos

9.
Links to pages that are even more boring than Facebook

**10.
People get killed in auto accidents
while posting on Facebook**

**This is known as permanently
un-friending oneself**

11.
THE USE OF CARTOON CHARACTERS FOR PROFILE PHOTOS

12.
Anything you say on Facebook can and will be used against you

13.
When people who are actually your friends ignore your friend request

14.
ENDLESS PHOTOS OF CHILDREN'S PLAY ACTIVITIES

15.
IT'S WHERE BLOGGERS GO TO DIE

16.
Annoying ads for stuff Facebook is sure you want but you actually don't

**17.
Incessant use of Bible quotes by people who aren't particularly spiritual**

18.
Cameron Winklevoss

19.
Tyler Winklevoss

20.
There's no category for enemies

21.
Friends post photos of themselves on the beach in Maui when it's the middle of January

22.
It's like junior high all over again

23.
If you want to

something on Facebook you have to download an app

24.
It's more addicting than TV, but without the premium channels

25.

YOU RECEIVE 238 HAPPY BIRTHDAY MESSAGES AND THEY ALL EXPECT YOU TO COMMENT

26.
Relentless use of the word *awesome* for things that aren't

27.
THE SAME GOES FOR THE WORD *AMAZING*

28.
And the word *incredible*

29.
Because what happens in Vegas no longer stays in Vegas

30.
**YOU DISCOVER THAT
YOUR HIGH SCHOOL EX TURNED OUT
MUCH BETTER LOOKING
THAN THE PERSON YOU ARE
CURRENTLY WITH**

31.
Tagging
(a practice best confined to games of "it" or professional wrestling)

32.
Update envy

33.
FRIENDS WHO POST EMBARRASSING DETAILS ABOUT THEIR LIFE AND EXPECT YOU TO COMMENT

34.
Farmville

35.
People who insist on letting you know their whereabouts at all times. "Waiting in line at Starbucks. Dry cleaner next. Then home."

36.

EVERYBODY ELSE ON THE SITE SEEMS TO BE HAVING MORE FUN THAN YOU'RE HAVING

**37.
You're scared about
what Facebook might do
with all the information
they have about you**

38.
Every member of Congress has a Facebook page

39.
THREADS THAT NEVER DIE

40.
Timelines!

41.
Old college friends posting about how you only got pity sex back then

42.
Your privacy settings don't really ensure your privacy

43.
Facebook has become Twitter with photos

44.
Facebook has become Pinterest with captions

45.
People on Facebook never met a sunset they didn't like

46.
You receive invitations to events on the day of the event

47.
PEOPLE BUGGING YOU BECAUSE YOU IGNORED THE INVITATION

48.
Photos of dogs and cats with word balloons telling you what the animal is supposed to be thinking

49.

IT'S ALWAYS SOMEBODY'S BIRTHDAY

50.
One of your friends posts on your wall that you used to eat paste in third grade

51.
Endless reminders

52.
ENDLESS UPDATES

53.
Donald Trump will gladly accept your friend request, but try asking him for a loan

54.
Mark Zuckerberg is a billionaire and he says he doesn't even like money

55.
GROUP PHOTOS
WHERE YOU DON'T KNOW
ANY OF THE PEOPLE

56.
Lindsey Lohan has more "Likes" than Buddha

57.
The lowest paid employee of Facebook makes more than most teachers

58.
Celebrities don't do their own posts

59.
RANTS ABOUT LIBERALS

60.
RANTS ABOUT CONSERVATIVES

61.
Photos of friends graduating from colleges you couldn't get into

62.
Just because you have
lots of Facebook friends in
common with someone, it
doesn't mean you have anything
else in common with them

63.
**There's a very real chance
you could run into someone whose
friend request you ignored**

64.
Even though she accepts your friend request ScarJo won't really be your friend

65.
**BEING TOLD EVERY NIGHT
WHAT YOUR FRIENDS ARE HAVING
FOR DINNER**

66.
Someone you've been hiding from for years finds you

67.

IT'S EASIER TO GET OUT OF THE MOB THAN IT IS TO CLOSE YOUR FACEBOOK ACCOUNT

68.
Photos of your friends standing next to hot cars while you drive a piece of crap

69.

SOONER OR LATER, YOU'LL RUN INTO THE PERSON YOU LOST YOUR VIRGINITY TO

70.
You poke, but don't get poked back

71.
People who have
no opinions in real life suddenly
become know-it-alls

72.

Sports fans who tell you exactly how they'd do it if they were the coach

73.
The more trivial the matter, the more likely it is to be posted

74.
OBSCURE PHOTOS WITHOUT CAPTIONS

75.
Obscure captions without photos

76.
It's way too easy to get caught cheating on your mate

77.

SHARED PHOTOS

OF UNAPPETIZING FOOD

78.
Idiotic contests

79.
Friends who post details about their dog's day

80.
People who friend
and then un-friend.

This is called doing
an aboutfacebook

81.
Weather updates from people who don't live in your area

82.
RELIGIOUS ZEALOTS
WHO TRY
TO CONVERT YOU

83.
You're depressed all day because no one liked your comment

**84.
People who pat themselves
on the back for every little thing:
"I was a great dad today; I played
catch with Jimmie for 15 minutes."**

85.
Photos of great looking food from restaurants you can't afford to visit

86.
Non-parents dispensing child-rearing advice

87.
After poking what comes next; groping?

88.

INVITATIONS TO EVENTS YOU'RE NOT INTERESTED IN ATTENDING

89.
"People you may know" is generally made up of people you don't know or people you do know and don't want as friends

90.
Icky sticky love notes:
"Brad, you're the peas
to my carrots on
the dinner plate of love."

91.
PEOPLE WHO BOAST ABOUT THEIR CHILD'S LESS THAN STELLAR ACCOMPLISHMENTS:
"PETE JR. GOT 5TH PLACE IN THE MIDDLE SCHOOL SCIENCE FAIR. MIT HERE WE COME!!!"

92.

FRIENDS WHO MAKE YOU FEEL GUILTY IF YOU MISS A DAY OF POSTING

93.
Where else would a person talk about cleaning out their friends

94.
Friends from college who send a friend request and end up trying to sell you life insurance

95.
Or worse,
vitamin supplements

96.
Or even worse;
weight loss programs

97.
CONSPIRACY THEORISTS

98.
Friends who post
hourly health reports:
"I woke up with a
stiff neck; Took 2 Tylenol.
Better now."

99.
YOUR PARENTS GET OFFENDED WHEN YOU REFUSE THEIR FRIEND REQUEST BECAUSE THERE ARE THINGS YOU DON'T WANT THEM TO KNOW

100.
Friends who post lyrics to their favorite song on your wall and expect you to fill in the next verse

101.
You're only as cool as your latest update

www.ingramcontent.com/pod-product-compliance
Lightning Source LLC
Chambersburg PA
CBHW071312040426
42444CB00009B/1983